German

WORLD WAR II

REENACTING

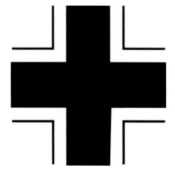

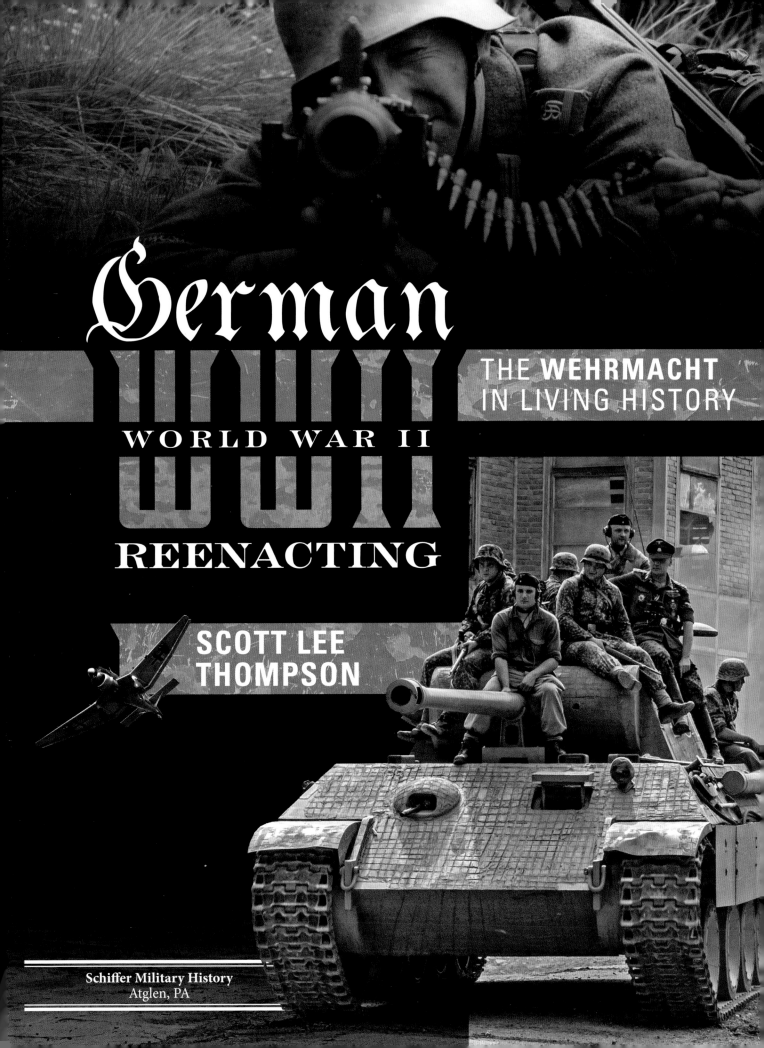

German

WORLD WAR II

REENACTING

THE **WEHRMACHT**
IN LIVING HISTORY

SCOTT LEE THOMPSON

Schiffer Military History
Atglen, PA

Dedicated to reenactors everywhere,
and the men and women they portray.

Printed in China
ISBN: 978-0-7643-4889-1

We are interested in hearing from authors with book ideas on related topics.

Published by Schiffer Publishing Ltd.
4880 Lower Valley Road
Atglen, PA 19310
Phone: (610) 593-1777
FAX: (610) 593-2002
E-mail: Info@schifferbooks.com.

Visit our web site at: www.schifferbooks.com
Please write for a free catalog. This book may be purchased from the publisher. Try your bookstore first.

CONTENTS

PREFACE

This book gives the reader a feel for what it is like to portray a World War II German soldier and, in the process, understand how those soldiers fought, lived, ate, slept, and, if they were lucky, survived. It does not describe the details and history of any of the machines, weapons, vehicles, or other items used by the reenactors. They are covered in depth in many other volumes.

Few armies in history have carried the mystique of the German Wehrmacht of WWII. When reenactors started holding World War II events, many were drawn to portray the tough German combat soldier and the deadly and efficient weapons with which he fought.

Modern-day reenactors have created a bewildering array of units portraying different divisions and combat groups. Huge amounts of money have been spent importing, restoring, and even hand-building wartime vehicles. When the hobby began to take off in the mid-1970s, reenactors were forced to modify Swedish uniforms, East German boots, and make do with whatever weapons and gear were available that "looked the part."

As the hobby grew and thousands of WWII history fans swelled the ranks, businesses began to crop up making authentic reproductions of uniforms, replica weapons, and gear. When Germany re-armed in the 1950s, factories began producing the same equipment they had made in the war-time years, so those mess kits, belts, canteens, and other gear can be roughed up in the field instead of priceless originals.

Individual groups portray actual German units, paying careful attention to authenticity and detail, right down to the chain of command. Reenactors often start out as privates and can rise to different ranks and responsibility. Public events include weapons displays and demonstrations, as well as mock battles to give the public a glimpse of "how it was."

Some members have sunk fortunes into original tanks, half tracks, and even airplanes. The common bond among reenactors is the love of history, and the desire that it not be forgotten. The combat soldiers of all nations are represented and, world-wide, the events give people a priceless opportunity to see one of the most important events of the twentieth century come to life.

It is my hope that this book will give the reader some idea of the unbelievable work, dedication, and expense undertaken by thousands of living history fans around the world.

It is the purpose of this book to give the reader a time machine with which to go back and see WWII in living color, through the miracle of modern photography and the herculean efforts of the reenactors. Photos were chosen that portrayed the German soldier's life. Not all the impressions will be 100% perfect or authentic, but I hope they open a window into history in order to give the reader a feeling of being there.

INFANTRY

Die Infanterie—the backbone of the Wehrmacht, or any other army—is usually the first choice when becoming a reenactor. The German army was one of the most highly trained and motivated armed forces in history. In the beginning, around 1975, reenactors had to make do with modified modern equipment. Today, a horde of vendors produce uniforms and gear to equip an authentic German soldier.

Above: Waffen SS march in their distinctive cammo uniforms. **Below:** Army motorcycle and cavalry recon.

Above: Waffen SS troop formation. **Below:** Guarding the roast pig, with Pak 40 anti-tank gun in background.

Above: Gross Deutschland troops disembark from a convoy under the barrel of an MG42 machine gun.
Below: Gross Deutschland Soldaten in winter gear prepare to support a Tiger I tank in an attack.

Above: Heer (Army) troops with K-98 rifles, and on the left, a Beretta M-38 submachine gun.
Below: 2. Panzerdivision troops adjusting gear prior to a battle. Note the MG34 machine gun on the Lafette heavy mount.

Above: An MG42 gunner waits in his bunker. **Below:** Setting up camp; an Opel Blitz truck is in the background.

German Fallschirmjäger (paratroops) in their distinctive helmets and jump smocks. In the second half of the war, they were used mainly as ground troops. The man at right (below) carries the MG42 machine gun.

Many reenactors prefer to portray German officers. There is a wide variety of impressions to choose from, from anonymous officers of Heer (army), Luftwaffe (air force), Kriegsmarine (navy), and Waffen SS, to famous characters like Erwin Rommel, Heinz Guderian, and Eric Von Manstein.

When properly done in coordination with a unit, inspections by these fellows can be impressive, as well as a little intimidating.

Above: German Soldaten on the Ostfront near Orachev being given orders and preparing to move out.
Below: Note the variety of field gear carried by the German soldier on the versatile "Y-strap" suspenders: a mess kit, zeltbahn (shelter quarter), gas mask cannister, bread bag, and a canteen are present.

Above: Stacking rifles under the watchful eye of the commander. **Below:** A mixed battle group (**Kampfgruppe**). The man at center carries the deadly "Panzerschreck," the 8.8cm German version of the bazooka.

Above: Street fighting. Note the MG42s set up on the Dreibein (tripod) and with the bipod at right.
Below: Troops marching past a German factory. Note the Type 87 Volkswagen command car.

WAFFENFABRIK

Above: "Feldpost," or mail call, is the time all soldiers live for. A letter, or better yet a package from home, is the next best thing to going home for lonely, war-weary soldiers. Below: A column stops in the woods.

PANZERS

Panzer divisions were the heart and soul of Blitzkrieg, or lightning war. In the early years of WWII, the Panzers smashed through all opposition as a premier offensive weapon. As the war turned against Germany, the Panzers proved to be equally deadly on the defensive. Original German tanks are extremely rare. The few that survived the cutting torch are in museums. It's truly a rarity to see an original Panzer operating under its own power. Many static displays are built using stationary museum Panzers. Reenactors also go to great expense to recreate German tanks using modern donor vehicles. The Panzer will always be the most sought-after vehicle in the reenacting hobby, with original vehicles worth millions of dollars.

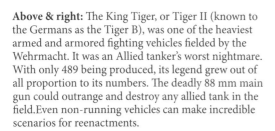

Above & right: The King Tiger, or Tiger II (known to the Germans as the Tiger B), was one of the heaviest armed and armored fighting vehicles fielded by the Wehrmacht. It was an Allied tanker's worst nightmare. With only 489 being produced, its legend grew out of all proportion to its numbers. The deadly 88 mm main gun could outrange and destroy any allied tank in the field.Even non-running vehicles can make incredible scenarios for reenactments.

A beautifully restored early-war, Czech-made Panzer 38(t).

The sleek and deadly Jagdpanther tank destroyer with 88mm gun. Note the size of these large vehicles!

There are only a few dozen German tanks left in the world, and most of them are in museums. With the scarcity and high price of actual Panzers, it's no wonder many reenactors have gone to great time and expense to recreate them from donor vehicles.

This Tiger I, boasting six kill rings, has been built on the chassis of a Russian T-55 main battle tank. The only real difference between this vehicle and the original are the tracks and road wheels. Tigers, Panthers, and Sturmgeschütz III assault guns have all been built on more modern vehicles.With the slim chance of original Panzers taking the field anytime soon, this is a very viable alternative.

Above: An original Panther A, complete with Kubelwagen and accordion!

Above: The same Panther "A" in another setting. Note the Flak 38 20mm anti-aircraft gun at left.
Below: A Panzer IV with various other German vehicles in the background.

Above: Panther "A" with Sf l47 "Donkey-ear" binoculars and tripod, and a R-36 range finder on the ground.
Below: Beautifully reproduced Tiger I, right down to the interleaved road wheels. Hard to tell it's not real!

This Panther "A," parked in a German camp, sports **Zimmeritt** anti-magnetic mine paste.

Above: A strongpoint guarded by a Panzer IV. Note the Panzerschreck at the ready.
Below: Waffen SS troops and an army Kamerad confer under the watchful eye of their Panzerkampfwagen IV.

The Hetzer tank destroyer was introduced later in the war. Built on the reliable Panzer 38-T chassis, it was an effective little vehicle built for ambush tactics.

The presence of real German armor made a big impression in reenacting. Many Hetzers were sold to other nations after the war, and survived to make reenactments more historically authentic.

Above: Reproduction Panzer III with a long 50mm gun. **Below:** Repro Panzer III with a short 7.5 cm main gun.

Above: A reproduction Sturmgeschütz in a German convoy. **Below:** Sturmgeschütz (**StuG**) with 7.5cm gun.

Above: A reproduction Panther carrying Panzergrenadiers. This vehicle is built on the Russian T-55 chasssis.
Below: The Panther passes a war-time German weapons factory or "**Waffenfabrik**."

Above: Original Panzer III with a long-barreled 50mm main gun.
Below: A beautifully reproduced StuG III with the correct six road wheels and long main 7.5 cm gun. Note the 3.7cm Flak gun in the background.

Above: The legendary Tiger I from the Bovington Tank Museum in Great Britain. This monster is always a show stopper. The repro StuG III in the background makes a nice scene, plus adds an idea of the Tiger I's size.

Above: The Germans made extensive use of "**Beutepanzer,**" or captured tanks like this Sherman.
Below: Another reproduction StuG III with "Schürzen" side skirts to defeat anti-tank weapons.

I couldn't resist adding a shot of this beautiful reproduction of the WWI German A7V Panzer! A fully functioning replica, it shows the progress made since the creation of this tank, the grandfather of German Panzer forces.

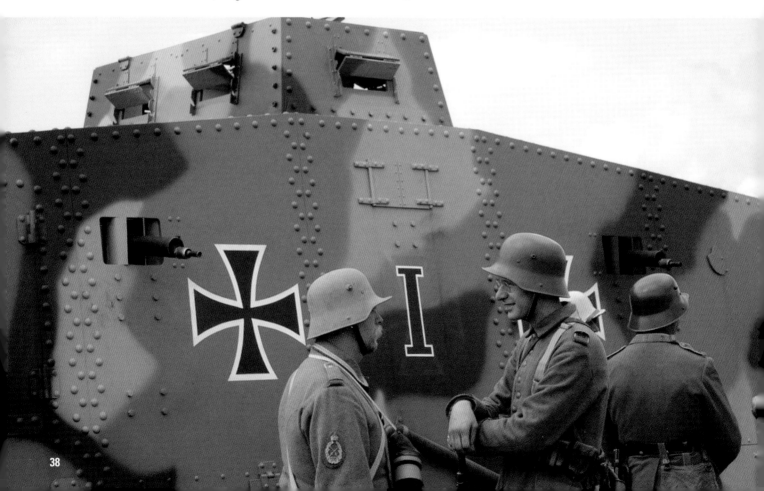

A Marder III Ausf. H tank destroyer scouts the terrain with the aid of supporting Panzergrenadiers.

Marder III "H" in action with Wehrmacht troops.

A Marder driver checks the map and the advance resumes. Troops are wearing splinter pattern cammo smocks.

Above and below: Reproduction SdKfz 222 and 232 armored cars.

Above: Paint job in the field. **Below:** SdKfz 247 leading the armored column.

Above: Maintenance of the 247 while troops practice rifle drill. Below: 247 interior. Note the MP40.

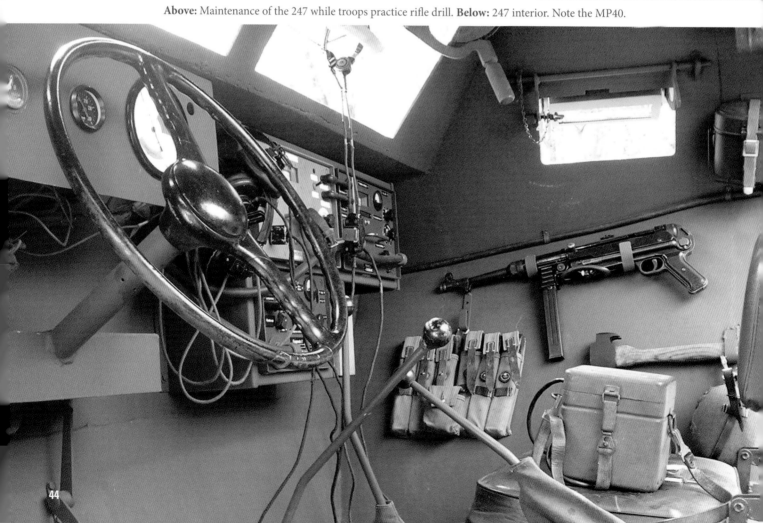

Reproduction 222 armored cars with 20mm cannon.

HALF-TRACKS

The SdKfz 251 half-track, built by Hanomag, was the backbone of the German Panzergrenadier, or armored infantry. After the war, Czechoslovakia continued to build a very similar version, the OT-810. Reenactors have re-worked these to the correct German appearance, through a large amount of work.

These lightly armored half-tracks deliver infantry safely to the battlefield. It's a thrill for the crowd to see these machines roar onto the field and discharge battle-ready combat troops.

Two model "C" vehicles with clam-shell doors are represented above. A model "D" is shown at right.

Above: A reproduction of a SdKfz 251 Model "D" belonging to 2. Panzerdivision. **Below:** A SdKfz 251 of the Grossdeutschland division.

Above: A Demag SdKfz 10 1-ton half-track. **Below:** A Sdkfz 251 D conversion passes through spring countryside.

A Demag 10 mounting a Russian 7.6 cm gun.

49

Above: A Sdkfz 251 C with 37mm gun at speed. Below: A Sdkfz 251 D medical half-track.

Above and below: A SdKfz 251 D with mounted 7.5cm Pak. 40.

Above: Another medical SdKfz 251 half-track. **Below:** Consulting with the driver of an Opel Blitz.

A **Maultier** (German for "mule") half-track on a Ford truck chassis with a Bren gun carrier undercarriage.

KETTENKRAD

The Kettenkrad half-track motorcycle is one of the most readily recognizable German vehicles. Made famous in the movie *Saving Private Ryan*, it was another rugged, versatile vehicle that served well on all fronts. It is also fun to drive and ride in.

Reenactors fortunate enough to have one of these machines in their unit can pull light artillery, lay telephone wire, or just make a tour of the grounds. Of course, routine maintenance is necessary to keep the "Krad" running smoothly. Here, the "Krad" is being worked on for electrical trouble under the careful eye of the **Leutnant** (lieutenant).

Above: Hooking up to a 20mm Flak 38 anti-aircraft gun. This was an ideal load for the tough little vehicle. **Below:** The Kettenkrad was not meant for combat operations, but sometimes it can't be avoided!

RAUPPENSCHLEPPER OST

The Rauppenschlepper Ost, or "RSO," is a rare sight on the reenacting battlefield. This versatile vehicle was a response to the horrific road conditions on the Russian front. Lovingly restored, this RSO is hauling a PAK 40 anti-tank gun. One of a reenactor's biggest thrills is to ride on an original German vehicle.

There were never enough of these popular vehicles to go around, and the German soldier, more often than not, struggled along on foot or alongside equally miserable draft animals. The trees give cover from Allied air forces.

Original war-time Opel Blitz trucks in action. These trucks were truly the backbone of the Wehrmacht.

The Opel Blitz ("Blitz" means "Lightning" in German) was rugged and reliable, and built in both 2 and 4-wheel drive versions.

Although many other models of truck were used, including domestic, foreign, and captured, the Blitz is always right at home on a German reenactment field. The Blitz above sports an original war-time canvas tarp.

At right, an MG34 machine gun team dismounts from the Blitz.

Infantryman's motto: "It's always better to ride!" The Wehrmacht never came close to being fully motorized.

Service on the Eastern front. The Russian winter severely tested even reliable trucks like the Opel Blitz.

Evacuating wounded into the reliable Opel Blitz truck. The wounded man keeps a grip on his Stg44 rifle.

Opel Blitz with Flak 38

This 20mm Flak 38 anti-aircraft gun has been mounted on a 1945 Opel Blitz truck. The truck is rare, because it has the late-war wooden cab, used to save valuable resources.

This greatly increased the mobility of these guns, and increased their survival rate, as they were quicker to move out of sight of roving allied fighter-bombers and artillery.

This Flak 38 is equipped with original ammunition boxes and accessories.

63

The German Volkswagen Type 82 "**Kubelwagen**," or "bucket car," was the German equivalent of the U.S. Jeep. Although it was not a 4-wheel drive vehicle, it was rugged and got where it wanted to go, due to its light weight and high clearance.

These rare vehicles add enormously to the atmosphere of a reenactment, as they were everywhere, in every theater. Few things look more impressive than a German officer being driven by his adjutant in an original Kubelwagen.

Restoring Kubelwagens involves finding original parts, from tires to lights to war-time tools and gas cans.

The German national flag was used for identification by friendly aircraft from early to mid-war.

Consulting officers gather around a Volkswagen Kubelwagens in front of a distillery. Nice choice! "**Abstand 30m**" means the distance between vehicles in a convoy should be 30 meters.

The Horch heavy field car was a heavy duty, four-wheel-drive vehicle that was used to carry troops, light artillery, and anti-tank weapons. Rugged and well-built, it makes a great weapons carrier in reenactments.

The example below is shown hauling the Pak36 3.7 anti-tank gun.

Above: A Mercedes Benz Be L1500A Kfz 40. **Below:** A "BMW" Stoewer R200 with a soldier "under the hood."

Above: A Mercedes Benz W31 G4 with staff officers. Below: A BMW-built Stoewer R200 on the move.

Above: A Mercedes Benz Be L1500A Kfz 40 with 2cm Flak 38. **Below:** An Opel Blitz van body truck.

Above: A Mercedes Benz Be L1500A Kfz 40 with twin-mounted MG42s. **Below:** A Volkswagen Type 87.

Above: A Krupp L2 H143 "**Schnauzer**" with Flak 30 2cm. **Below:** A Mercedes Benz with a Pak 40 7.5cm.

Above: The amphibious Schwimmwagen featured 4WD and was very popular with the troops.

Above: The driver's position. Note the "**Verbandkasten**" (first aid kit).

Motorrad

The German army used an amazing variety of military motorcycles, the most well-known being the BMW series. War-time bikes, like the BMW R75 above, command a fortune. Fortunately, the Russians and Chinese produced post-war copies of the BMW R-71 series, which are easily converted to very convincing German WWII motorcycles.

This way, reenactors don't worry about tearing up an original $40,000 bike in the field. The BMW plant was moved—bricks, machinery, and employees—to Ukraine, where they continued to build them.

Above: A German column begins a night march.
Below: Just as in war time, plenty of things go wrong.

Much of the German army was horse-drawn and bicycle-mounted throughout the war.

FLAK 88mm

The legendary 88! Just the mention of the name alone was enough to give the jitters to any Allied soldier. Equally versatile at taking on tanks or airplanes, it cut its teeth in the Spanish Civil War and became a legend on the sands of Africa with Erwin Rommel. This remarkable Flak battery recreation is ready for action.

The crew prepares for firing. The soldier with the "Scherenfernrohr" (scissors binoculars) finds the range.

Above: Along with the Flak "Acht-Acht" (88) is a Fiesler Storch. Note the gun trailer at right. **Below:** Feuer!

The Flak 38 was a 20mm anti-aircraft gun. With a rate of fire of 220 RPM and effective range of 5,000 yards, it was a comfort to have on-hand, and an absolute necessity, as the Germans lost air superiority on virtually every front. Many are available, having served in many armies post-war.

Above: A Flak 38 in action; note the net "empty brass" catcher. Below: A Flak 38 mounted on an Opel Blitz.

A 37mm Flak gun. Built mainly for export to allies, it was also used by the Wehrmacht, especially in the east.

PAK 40

The PAK 40 is a 75mm anti-tank gun introduced to handle heavily armored opponents, such as the Russian T-34. The restored gun, above, fires black powder, and the ground shakes when the gunner fires.

This is the same gun that was mounted on the Panzer IV and Marder III. You get an appreciation for the gun's power, seeing it in use. Most German guns are now adapted to fire black powder or are gas-adapted.

Above: Feuer! Hearing protection is a must. Below: 2. Panzerdivision Kampfgruppe.

The 3.7cm PAK 36 was Germany's light anti-tank gun. It was referred to as the "Door Knocker" later in the war, due to its lack of effect on later Allied armor.

Below: The crew hurriedly withdraws in the face of an advancing Sexton tank.

INFANTRY GUN IG18

This IG18 "Light Infantry Gun" is part of the Midwest's 2. Panzerdivision. It is in action here at a tactical battle in an American Midwest reenactment. At the top, it is being hauled by an original Opel Blitz truck.

At "tacticals," reenactors hold battles with no public present, for maximum realism. Umpires decide who has "taken a hit." The two sides will often have goals of capturing enemy headquarters and strongpoints. The IG18 is a light, maneuverable weapon to have on hand, with a range of 3,880 yards.

Above: A 7.5cm infantry gun on rubber tires. **Below:** An infantry gun with wooden wheels being prepared to fire.

Original le.F. H. 18, 105mm cannon in firing position. These pieces were the backbone of Wehrmacht artillery.

The German field kitchen, or "Gulaschkanone" (Goulash cannon), was an indispensable part of the German army. Hungry soldiers didn't fight for long, so the presence of a field kitchen adds a great deal of authenticity to a reenactment.

When the troops get to eat from the same field kitchen the original veterans ate from, they get a literal taste of a soldier's life. The field kitchen above left was designed for infantry and was pulled with horses. Some (above right and below) were for motorized units, and were pulled by trucks.

Above: Serving troops. Note the "Fleischwolf" (meat grinder). Below: A field kitchen for motorized units.

Above: A 1939, horse-drawn, infantry field kitchen. Below: This 1943 field kitchen has an integral roaster.

The Wehrmacht used over seven million horses during WWII. Their presence at reenactments adds authenticity to the event, depicting a time in which artillery, wagons, and supplies were often horse-drawn.

Besides using a vast number of horses for transport, the Germans also made great use of mounted cavalry, who could traverse terrain inaccessible for even tracked vehicles or four-wheel drive.

Pyrotechnics add to the reality of reenacting. Explosions simulate artillery barrages and bring home the horror of war. Reenacting honors real heros who fought and died. It is not just a fun hobby.

Panzergrenadiers advance under firing support from a Marder III Ausf. H.

Above: A Russian T-34 burns after a hit by a Panzerfaust anti-tank rocket. **Below:** "For you, the war is over!"

Above: Tactical battles, where the public is not in attendance, are the closest thing to truly experiencing combat. Soldiers who have been "hit" will remove their helmet and retire from the battlefield for a specified period of time, only to return as a "reinforcement."
Below: Extensive fortifications are sometimes built to represent everything from bunkers, to dragon's teeth, to ruined villages.

Winter battles test the resolve of reenactors, weapons, and equipment.

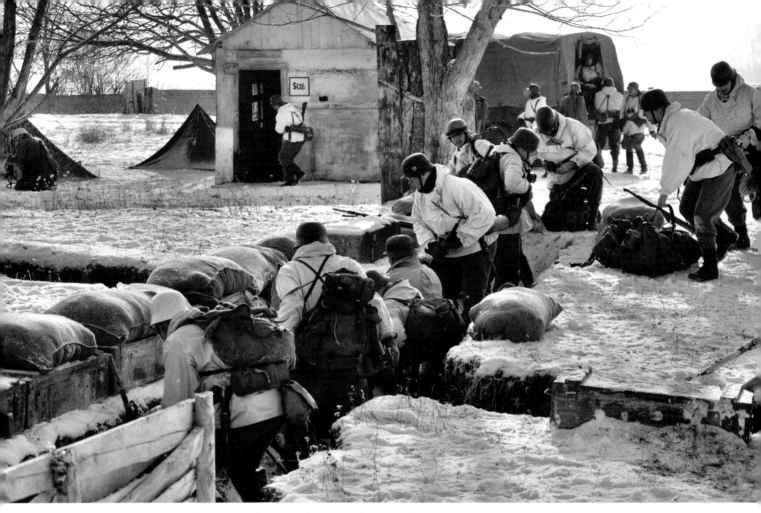

Above: Elaborate trench systems...hard work, but worth the effort. **Below:** A MG34 machine gun in action.

Above: Hand-to-hand combat with entrenching tools. **Below:** A MG 08 Maxim pressed into service late in the war.

Above: A "local" points out enemy troops. **Below:** Hit! Hopefully a **Sanitäter** (medical corpsman) is near.

Above: Armored support moves up. **Below:** Riflemen with K-98s on the firing line.

Above: The rare Sturmgewehr 44 gives added firepower. **Below:** A Gebirgsjäger (mountain troops) casualty.

Above: A 222 armored car moves up. **Below:** A 3.7cm PAK gun and half-track with Russian 7.6mm anti-tank gun.

Above: Tank hunting team with a Panzerschreck. **Below:** Fire support from a half-track with a mounted MG34.

Above: A German commander gives the signal to "move up!" **Below:** Dodging enemy fire.

PIRITUSFABRIK A.G.
Fr. Janicek – Syrowitz

Above: Clearing a Russian pillbox position with a "Panzerturm" mounted tank turret. Below: Kaputt!

Late in the war, a mixed group of Wehrmacht and Volksturm defend a German town with the help of a Panther. They secure American prisoners (**above**), then move to attack the American armor.

Above: A half-track brings reinforcements. **Below:** The Panther is knocked out and G.I.s advance.

Rest needs to be taken whenever and wherever it can be, whether on the hard ground or in a motorcycle sidecar.

Above: A satisfying drink from a "**Feldflasche**" (canteen) after setting up the Zeltbahn four-man tent.
Below: Novels and humorous books like *Front Soldaten Lachen* (front-line soldier laughs) were very popular.

Above: Exhausted soldiers, like this mortar crew, took advantage of any chance to catch some shut-eye.
Below: The "**Mundharmonika**" (harmonica) was popular with the music-loving Germans.

Simple joys, like a game of chess or Skat, helped get the mind off the reality of war. Division newspapers also kept soldiers informed of the "big picture," colored as the news might be, and were read ravenously.

Sports and games were very important for the morale of the Soldaten. Many reenactors go so far as to organize their own sports teams, complete with period uniforms.

Above: Sometimes troops were billeted with local families and shared each other's bounty, from cigarettes and chocolate to freshly caught game.
Below: Music, like this impromptu concert, was an important pastime.

TRANSPORTATION

Many German divisions traveled by train, for both speed and to save wear and tear on vehicles. These reenactors have recreated a motorized unit loaded on railroad cars, awaiting the move to the front.

Crews loaded, secured, and stayed on the car with their vehicles. Often, Zeltbahn tents were erected for protection from the elements. If they were lucky enough to have a vehicle with a canvas top, all the better!

These young Waffen SS troops, waiting to move, display the camouflaged clothing that was pioneered by the Waffen SS. Many post-war countries studied the patterns intensely and adapted many of the ideas.

This soldier wears an Italian Camo pattern Heer (army) jacket with fur lining. His helmet has been painted in a rough finish to avoid reflecting sunlight.

Above: The train begins to unload and the division begins the time-consuming task of reorganizing. The men in the car above wait their turn.
Below: The engine backs up and prepares for the return trip.

An excellent communications network often gave the Wehrmacht an edge over the enemy. War-time radios are expensive and hard to find. Reenactors have done a great job restoring and equipping themselves with German radio equipment and telephone systems.

These extra touches of realism make for a truly believable set piece. Some go as far as bringing the equipment back to operational status and using them in the field.

Above: Sometimes the best form of communication is to have a look for yourself.
Below: Elaborate sets of German transmitters, receivers, radios, and typewriters recreate German communication centers.

Above: The **R36 Entfernungsmesser** range finder was used for artillery and anti-aircraft guns.
Below: The **Scherenfernrohr Sf-l4Z** "Donkey Ears" scissors optics were used to observe and find the range for ground targets.

Above: Forward observers use working Wehrmacht field telephones to keep in touch with rear areas.
Below: Even elaborate observation towers are put into use to keep an eye on enemy forces.

Above: Personal cameras were plentiful during the war and millions of photos were taken by soldiers.
Below: A very well thought-out communications/command tent.

In addition to static displays, the Germans also used an excellent series of mobile field radios, and reenactors are quick to take advantage of these gems when they find them.

The famous MG42 machine gun, the replacement for the intrepid MG34, was nicknamed "Hitler's Buzz Saw" for good reason. With a rate of fire of 1,200-1,500 rounds per minute, it was the terror of the battlefield and made a sound like a giant tearing a bolt of cloth. The design of the gun was so perfect that even today, the same gun, virtually unchanged, is used by the modern German army and much of NATO.

Post-war copies are readily available and the roomy receiver lends itself to being gas-adapted. The sound of a full auto machine gun lends great authenticity to a reenactment. Oxygen and propane tanks are hidden in ammunition boxes, motorcycle sidecar tubs, or whatever vehicle is mounting the weapon.

Above: The business end of the MG42. Both live blank-firing and gas-adapted guns are used. Often the gun is a Yugoslavian M53 or modern German MG3, virtually identical to the wartime original.

Above: The number two gunner keeps a steady feed of belted ammunition to satisfy the MG 42's voracious appetite! Up to a five-man crew serviced the weapon. **Below:** Feuer frei!

Great care is taken in machinegun emplacements to protect the gunner from return fire.

Although the MG42 is a very robust gun, proper cleaning and maintenance was, and is, of great importance.

MG 34

The MG34 actually preceeded the MG42, had a lower rate of fire, and required more care and maintenance in the field, hence its replacement. They are a hard gun to find now, and a treasure at reenactments. It is seen here on the Lafette mount with optics in heavy machine gun mode.

Below: An MG34, on the Lafette mount in heavy machine-gun mode, is an accurate and deadly weapon.

Later in the war, obsolete guns, like this Maxim MG 1908/15, were pressed into service. This Luftwaffe field division unit has knocked out a Russian tank and the "Devil's Paintbrush" is providing covering fire.

PANZERSCHRECK

The German counterpart to the bazooka was actually designed after a captured American bazooka, and improved. It fired an 88mm rocket, which was fired electronically.

With the Panzerschreck and it's little brother, the Panzerfaust, the German infantryman finally had a fighting chance against tanks.

Most reenacting Panzerschrecks are reproductions and many are rigged to fire a blast of smoke from the rear, for realism, adding greatly to reenactments.

Right: Note the tank destruction badge on the shoulder of the man on the left. The soldier is adjusting the carrying strap while a rocket is removed from its box.

The Panzerfaust was a hand-held, disposable, anti-tank rocket and the forerunner of the RPG. Millions were produced. It can be fitted with realistic smoke effects to appear as though it is being fired.

MORTARS

Original and reproduction German 81mm mortars are fitted with devices to fire harmless bombs. Often a shotgun shell is used to produce the effect.

Germany's excellent main battle rifle and mainstay of the Wehrmacht, the Mauser K-98k is in good supply and widely used in renactments. From 1935 to 1945, over 14 milion were produced.

Germany's stamped metal masterpiece, the **Sturmgewehr 44**, or MP43, was the world's first assault rifle. It's a rare and sought-after weapon for reenacting. Reproductions are very expensive.

MP 38/40

Sometimes mistakenly called the "Schmeisser," the MP40 was the world's first successful submachine gun. The 9mm weapon is available for reenacting as original guns and blank firing reproductions.

Above: An exceedingly rare G41 semi-automatic rifle, and its replacement, the more successful G43.
Below: Germany's semi-automatic rifles never came close to replacing the bolt-action Mauser K-98.

The unsung heros of any army: the doctors, nurses, tailors, cobblers, etc. They kept the fighting machine running.

SUPPORT PERSONNEL

CHAPLAINS

Chaplains played a vital part in morale and the well-being of the soldiers. Germany was a very religious country, despite the depravity of much of its government. Most soldiers were Catholic or Protestant, and their needs were met by the Kriegspfarrer (war pastor).

Chaplains and church services in reenacting units play an important role in explaining what motivated the German soldier to carry on against impossible odds. Their belt buckle read, "**Gott mit uns**" (God with us), and most of them believed it.

No battlefield reenactment is authentic without the selfless medics and **Roten Kreuz** (Red Cross) nurses who saved hundreds of thousands of lives.

The next two pages depict the transfer of a wounded soldier by truck back to the field hospital.

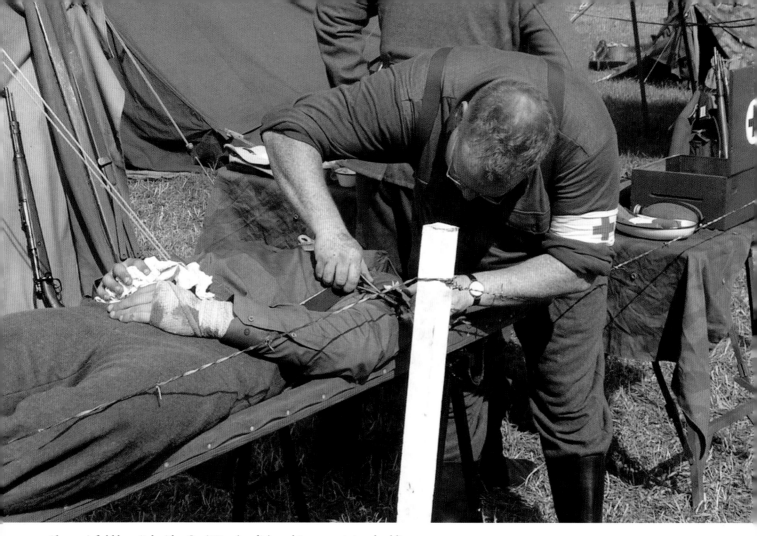

Above: A field hospital with a **Sanitäter** (medic) working on an injured soldier.
Below: "**Krankenschwestern**": German nurses and medical personnel of the **Rotes Kreuz,** or German Red Cross.

feldGendarmerie

An old German saying goes, "Ordnung muss sein!" (There must be order!) Thus, the military police!

MINES

Anti-tank Teller mines (**above**) and anti-personnel S-Mines (**below**) having their fuses set.

Often, reenactments are held at historic sites, recreating important events in the history of the war. Standing where "they stood" is a heady experience, allowing one to get even closer to history.

Sometimes the efforts of reenactors to recreate historic scenarios go completely out of this world, such as this reenactment that displayed, then blew up, a full-scale V2 rocket.

This fantastic recreation of a captured V-2 launch site was built at the War & Peace Show.

Luftwaffe reenactments are more rare, but no less important to history. Whether it's combat groups of Fallschimjäger or a vintage Messerschmitt Bf108 Taifun, this is an important arm of the German military.

Above: Messerschmitt Bf109. **Below:** The Ju52, nicknamed "Tante U" (Aunt Judi) or "Eiserne Annie" (Iron Annie).

A beautifully reproduced scene with a Fieseler Fi 156 Storch spotter plane.

Above: A Ju52 as a commercial Lufthansa airliner. **Below:** A Ju87 Stuka dive-bomber reproduction.

A remarkable U-Boat conning tower reproduction at the U.K.'s War & Peace Show.

My dear friend, Luftwaffe veteran Ed Reith, shows his collection of autographs from Me262 jet fighter pilots to a camp visitor.

German veterans, like all World War II participants, are getting scarcer every year. While they are still with us, they are God-sends to reenactors. Unlike Civil War reenactors, we can learn from the men and women who were actually there, because their advice is priceless. Besides their stories, they give advice about how to crew and handle weapons and vehicles, comment on the authenticity of uniforms and gear, and all that was worn and used.

German veterans are guests of honor at events, and often special dinners are held for them. When one of them passes from our midst, special funeral services are held, like the ones during the war. Usually, a wreath of oak branches is laid.

Reenactors make as much connection with these heroes as possible. We are blessed by their friendship and insight.

"Ein Prost!" Reenactors and veterans raise their glasses in celebration at an authentic German bar.

Prost! 2. Panzerdivision veteran Wolfgang Kloth enjoys "ein Glas Bier."

Many reenactors choose an individual soldier to portray. Whether he is a relative or a figure known only to them from the pages of history, this connection brings authenticity to reenacting and a strong desire to accurately portray the person chosen.

It's very rare to meet the person you portray! Pictured are original Gross Deutschland 7th Kompanie Hauptmann Herr Wachenagle (**above left**) and reenactor Robert Lawrence (**above right**), who portrays the Hauptman in the same reenacting Kompanie.

They are shown enjoying a conversation in the Deutsch Haus Bier Garden, in Munster, Germany.

They enjoyed some excellent German beer and had a great laugh together. Herr Wachenagle gave Mr. Lawrence a signed, war-time photo of himself, pictured here at right. It was a rare treat to meet the original commander of the Kompanie. Herr Wachenagle was amazed at the reenacting pictures, since reenactments or observances of the war are nearly unheard of in Germany. The Hauptman (captain) was well over 6 1/2 feet tall. He passed away a year after their meeting. It was a precious and rare honor, indeed.

ACKNOWLEDGMENTS

I'd like to express my thanks to the many people who helped with this book. Thanks to the many reenactors who have helped me over the years, from my impression as a Panzergrenadier (**above, center**) to a field cook with my own original "Gulaschkanone." A special thank you to all the veterans, both American and German, who have been an invaluable help in cultivating and maintaining my interest in the Second World War. Especially the German veterans, with whom I've enjoyed many wonderful friendships over the years, by my writing to them through *Kameraden*, the German veterans' magazine. They have helped me understand and see things through their perspective. They are now looked down on, in many ways, in their own country. To me they are heroes; fighting for what they thought was right, and to protect their loved ones and homeland.

Special thanks to my dear friends, Wolfgang Kloth and Ed Reith, for your friendship and the priceless information you passed on to me.

Last, but not least, my heartfelt thanks to the many people who contributed their own photographs to this book. Without you, this project would not have been possible. You saved me traveling many thousands of miles around the world to record these important events.

Whether you are someone who reenacts or simply attends and enjoys the show, please continue. Without all of you, they will, as the old soldiers have, fade away; we can never allow that to happen.

Best regards,

Scott Lee Thompson

CONTRIBUTORS

The following people have made an invaluable contribution to this book by generously donating the use of their photos. Some have listed contact information.

Many, many thanks, my friends.

Scott Thompson

Aachen Stadt 1, Deutsches Roten Kreuz
www.Germanredcrossww2.com
Chris Devers
Kathryn Dobson
www.flickr.com/photos/kathrynruthd
William Dolak
Peter M. Garwood
pete_garwood@yahoo.com, Ipswich, England
Liz Gould
lizgould@btopenworld.com
Jeff Harrington
Bob Lawrence
www.grossdeutschland.com
rlawren3@optonline.net
Mark R. Lenz
http://www.flickr.com/photos/ddaybuff/
Craig Lindsey
http://www.flickr.com/photos/csl2112
Christopher J. Madeira
cm@cydera.com
Mark Milham
Matt Medlin
Dave Miller
Armchair Aviation Photography
armchair.aviator@yahoo.com Bay City, Michigan
Raymond Moore
nilkin67@mac.com
http://www.flickr.com/photos/nilkin67/
David A. Page
Simon Patrick
Panzer Fusilier Regiment Grossdeutschland.
www.germansoldier.co.uk
Marcus Price
http://www.flickr.com/photos/rikdom/
Mick Riggs
mickd23@firehousemail.com
Bob Sarnowski
mmsibob@comcast.net
http://paintedsoldier.weebly.com

Richard Sheehan
80 Clay St # 703, Quincy, MA 02170
Mick Stewart
pegasusatwar@gmail.com
www.pegasusatwar.com
Dave Stickland
(Flickr Username: John Lilburne)
David Stradal
Brett Stringer
Charlie Trumpess, The War Years
www.thewaryears.co.uk
Thomas Tutchek
Steven Whitehead
www.swhiteheadimages.co.uk
swhiteheadimages@aol.com
C & P Wray - 21st Panzer Division LHG
www.panzer21.com

PHOTO CREDITS

Cover: Top: Mark Milham.
   Bottom left: Author
   Bottom right: Jeff Harrington
Page 2. Dave Stickland
Page 4. Author.
Page 5: Jeff Harrington
Page 6: Simon Patrick
Page 7. Author.
Page 8. Top: Author.
   Bottom: C&P Wray.
Page 9. Top: Mick Riggs
   Bottom: Bill Dolak.
Page 10. Top: Mick Riggs
   Bottom: Dave Stradal.
Page 11. Bob Lawrence.
Page 12. Top: Dave Miller.
   Bottom: Author.
Page 13. Top: David A. Page
   Bottom: Author.
Page 14. Steve Whitehead.
Page 15. Liz Gould.
Page 16. Thomas Tutchek.
Page 17. Thomas Tutchek.
Page 18. Thomas Tutchek.
Page 19. Top: Author.
   Bottom: Bob Lawrence.
Page 20. Military Images.
Page 21. Peter Garwood.
Page 22. Top: Peter Garwod.
   Bottom: Military Images.
Page 23. Top: Peter Garwood.
   Bottom: Brett Stringer
Page 24. Marcus Price.
Page 25. Top: Mark Milham.
   Bottom: Charlie Trumpess.
Page 26. Top: Charlie Trumpess.
   Bottom: Dave Stickland.
Page 27. Top: Charlie Trumpess.
   Bottom: Brett Stringer.
Page 28. Thomas Tutchek.
Page 29. Top: Mick Riggs.
   Bottom: Steve Whitehead.
Page 30. Author.
Page 31. Top: Mark Milham.
   Bottom: Kathryn Dobson.
Page 32. Top: Bob Lawrence.
   Bottom: Mick Riggs.
Page 33. Thomas Tutchek.

Page 34. Top: Marcus Price.
   Bottom: Raymond Moore.
Page 35. Mick Riggs.
Page 36. Marcus Price.
Page 37. Top: Mark Milham.
   Bottom: Author.
Page 38. Marcus Price.
Page 39. C & P Wray.
Page 40. Top: Liz Gould.
   Bottom: C & P Wray.
Page 41. C & P Wray.
Page 42. Thomas Tutchek.
   Bottom: Author.
Page 43. Author.
Page 44. Author.
Page 45. Top: David Page.
   Bottom: Charlie Trumpess.
Page 46. Top: Marcus Price.
   Bottom: Author.
Page 47. Top: Author.
   Bottom: Bob Lawrence.
Page 48. Top: Author.
   Bottom: Thomas Tutchek.
Page 49. Thomas Tutchek.
Page 50. Top: Mark Milham.
   Bottom: Marcus Price.
Page 51. Thomas Tutchek.
Page 52. Thomas Tutchek.
Page 53. Author.
Page 54. Author.
Page 55. Author.
Page 56. Author.
Page 57. Author.
Page 58. Top: Author.
   Bottom: Thomas Tutchek.
Page 59. Thomas Tutchek.
Page 60. Thomas Tutchek.
Page 61. Author.
Page 62. Top: David Miller.
   Bottom: Author.
Page 63. Thomas Tutchek.
Page 64. Author.
Page 65. Top: Author.
   Bottom: Dave Miller.
Page 66. Top: Thomas Tutchek.
   Bottom: Author.
Page 67. Mark Milham
Page 68. Thomas Tutchek.

Page 69. Author.
Page 70. Thomas Tutchek.
Page 71. Top: Jeff Harrington.
   Bottom: Thomas Tutchek.
Page 72. Thomas Tutchek.
Page 73. Thomas Tutchek.
Page 74. Top: Mark Lenz.
   Bottom: Mark Milham.
Page 75. Top: Author.
   Bottom: Charlie Trumpess
Page 76. Thomas Tutchekk.
Page 77. Top: Thomas Tutchek.
   Bottom: Author.
Page 78. Author.
Page 79. Top: Bob Sarnowski.
   Bottom: Thomas Tutchek.
Page 80. **Top:** Mick Riggs.
   Bottom: Steven Whitehead.
Page 81. Top: David A. Page.
   Bottom: Author.
Page 82. Bob Lawrence.
Page 83. Author.
Page 84. Top: Jeff Harrington.
   Bottom: Ricard Sheehan
Page 85. Page 85. Jeff Harrington.
Page 86. Top: Chris Devers.
   Bottom: Jeff Harrington.
Page 87. Richard Sheehan.
Page 88. Steven Whitehead.
Page 89. Mark Milham
Page 90. Top: Author.
   Bottom: Thomas Tutchek.
Page 91. Top: Thomas Tutchek.
   Bottom: Dave Stickland.
Page 92: Top: Author.
   Bottom: Bob Sarnowski.
Page 93. Top: Author.
   Bottom: Steven Whitehead.
Page 94. Author.
Page 95. Top: Author.
   Bottom: Mick Riggs.
Page 96. Top: Bob Sarnowski.
   Bottom: Author.
Page 97. Thomas Tutchek.
   Bottom: Author.
Page 98. Thomas Tutchek.
Page 99. Author.
Page 100. Author.

PHOTO CREDITS

Page 101. Top: Steve Whitehead.
Bottom: Charlie Trumpess.
Page 102. Top: Author.
Bottom: Bob Lawrence
Page 103. Top: Author.
Bottom: Steve Whitehead.
Page 104. Author.
Page 105. Author.
Page 106. Author.
Page 107. Top: Author.
Bottom: Bob Sarnowski.
Page 108. Top: Bob Sarnowski.
Bottom: Richard Sheehan.
Page 109. Top: Author.
Bottom: David Stradal.
Page 110. Top: David Stradal.
Bottom: Simon Patrick.
Page 111. C & P Wray.
Page 112. Thomas Tutchek
Page 113. Thomas Tutchek
Page 114. Top: Simon Patrick.
Bottom: Thomas Tutchek.
Page 115. Thomas Tutchek.
Page 116. Thomas Tutchek.
Page 117. Thomas Tutchek.
Page 118. Top: Thomas Tutchek.
Bottom: Bob Sarnowski.
Page 119. Thomas Tutchek.
Page 120. Thomas Tutchek.
Page 121. Thomas Tutchek.
Page 122. Thomas Tutchek
Page 123. Thomas Tutchek.
Page 124. Thomas Tutchek.
Page 125. Thomas Tutchek.
Page 126. Thomas Tutchek.
Page 126. Thomas Tutchek.
Page 127. Thomas Tutchek.
Page 128. Mick Riggs.
Page 129. Author.
Page 130. Top: Bob Sarnowski.
Bottom: Simon Patrick.
Page 131. Simon Patrick.
Page 132. Top: Mark Lenz.
Bottom: Simon Patrick.
Page 133. Top: Steve Whitehead.
Bottom: Mark Lenz
Page 134. Top: Brett Stringer.
Bottom: Simon Patrick.

Page 135. Thoms Tutchek.
Page 136. Thomas Tutchek.
Page 137. Thomas Tutchek.
Page 138. Thomas Tutchek.
Page 139. Thomas Tutchek.
Page 140. Thomas Tutchek.
Page 141. Thomas Tutchek.
Page 142. Thomas Tutchek.
Page 143. Thomas Tutchek.
Page 144. Author.
Page 145. Top: Mick Riggs.
Bottom: Charlie Trumpess.
Page 146. Top: Author.
Bottom: Thomas Tutchek.
Page 147. Top: Simon Patrick.
Bottom: Thomas Tutchek.
Page 148. Thomas Tutchek.
Page 149. Top: Thomas Tutchek.
Botom: Richard Sheehan.
Page 150. Top: Brett Stringer.
Bottom: David Page.
Page 151. Top; Mark Milham.
Bottom: Chris Madeira.
Page 152. Top: Mick Riggs.
Page 153. Top: Simon Patrick.
Bottom: Marcus Price.
Page 154. Top: Bob Sarnowski.
Bottom: Bill Dolak.
Page 155: Author.
Page 156. Thomas Tutchek.
Bottom: Simon Patrcik.
Page 157. Thomas Tutchek.
Page 158. Author.
Page 159. Top: Mick Riggs.
Bottom: Author.
Page 160. Thomas Tutchek.
Page 161. Author.
Page 162. Top: Bob Sarnowski.
Bottom: Marcus Price.
Page 163. Top: Author.
Bottom: David Page
Page 164. Top: Bob Sarnowski.
Bottom: Author.
Page 165. Top: Simon Patrick.
Bottom: Bill Dolak.
Page 166. Top: Simon Patrick.
Bottom: Thomas Tutchek.

Page 167. Top: Simon Patrick.
Bottom: Bob Sarnowski.
Page 168. Top: Bob Lawrence.
Bottom: Bob Sarnowski.
Page 169. Top: Thomas Tutchek.
Bottom: Author.
Page 170. Mick Riggs.
Page 171. Top: Simon Patrick.
Bottom: Thomas Tutchek.
Page 172. Author.
Page 173. Author.
Page 174. Author.
Page 175. Top: Author.
Bottom: Aachen Stadt 1.
Page 176. Thomas Tucthek.
Page 177. Thomas Tutchek.
Page 178. Top: David Page.
Bottom: Aachen Stadt 1.
Page 179. Aachen Stadt 1.
Page 180. Top: Author.
Bottom: Thomas Tutchek.
Page 181. C & P Wray.
Page 182. C & P Wray.
Page 183. Mike Gilbert.
Page 184. Top: Mike Gilbert.
Bottom: Mick Riggs.
Page 185. Mick Riggs.
Page 186. Steve Whitehead.
Bottom: Charlie Trumpess.
Page 187. David Miller
Page 188. Top: Richard Sheehan.
Bottom: Jeff Harrington.
Page 189. Top: Steve Whitehead.
Bottom: Jeff Harrington.
Page 190. Top: Mick Riggs.
Bottom: Mark Milham.
Page 191. Author.
Page 192. Author.
Page 193. Bob Lawrence.
Page 194. Author.
Page 195. Author.
Page 196. Simon Patrick.
Page 199. Author.
Page 200. Author.

ABOUT THE AUTHOR

Scott Thompson was born in an era when all kids thought about was World War II. He started reenacting in 2002, as a Panzergrenadier, or armored infantryman. Always interested in cooking outdoors for large groups of people, he was lucky enough to find an original 1939 German field kitchen and became a company cook, or "Kuchenbull," with his original WWII Gulaschkanone (goulash cannon). He is author of *Gulaschkanone: The German Field Kitchen in WW2 & Reenacting*, president and a founder of the Central Illinois World War II Reenactors, Inc., and owns a Flak 38 20mm anti-aircraft gun. He may be reached at feldkoch@hughes.net

He resides in Illinois with his wife, Terry, and has a daughter, Bethany.